EDUCATION RESOURCE SERVICE
NORTH AYRSHIRE COUNCIL

FAMOUS PEOPLE
FAMOUS LIVES

Biographies of famous people to
support the curriculum.

Saint
Francis

by Emma Fischel
Illustrations by Nick Ward

W
FRANKLIN WATTS
NEW YORK•LONDON•SYDNEY

First published in 1999 by
Franklin Watts
96 Leonard Street
London
EC2A 4XD

Franklin Watts Australia
14 Mars Road
Lane Cove
NSW 2066

ISBN: 0 7496 3313 1

Dewey Decimal Classification Number: 270.092

A CIP catalogue record for this book
is available from the British Library.

Series editor: Sarah Ridley

Printed in Great Britain

Saint Francis

More than eight hundred years ago a baby boy was born in a place called Assisi, in Italy.

"I shall call him John," said his mother. "His father is away in France but he is sure to agree!"

He didn't though.

Francis wasn't born a saint.
People are made saints by the
Church after they die if they have
led a specially good and holy life.

But Francis wasn't even a specially good and holy child.

He DID learn all about God though.

The Church was very rich and powerful in those days.

People understood much less about their world and they looked to the Church for help.

Even tiny villages had a church, while in towns and cities cathedrals were built as big as castles.

7

Assisi was a big town with plenty of excitement going on and Francis was nearly always part of it.

His father was a cloth merchant. "You be one too," he said to Francis. "Lots of boys do the same job as their father."

But Francis didn't plan to be a cloth merchant. In fact, he didn't plan to be anything just yet.

Such a lively boy!

Towns were dirty, smelly places then. Beggars and pickpockets roamed the streets.

Fierce battles often raged between the different towns.

When Francis was twenty he fought for Assisi against a town called Perugia. He was taken prisoner and kept locked up for a whole year.

At last Francis was freed but
back home he fell dangerously
ill. It took him two years to
recover.

Francis set off once more to fight.
Then something happened that
changed his whole life.

At a place called Spoleto a voice
spoke to him. "Go home," said
the voice. "Await the call to
serve."

Francis started to look around him. "So many poor and needy," he said. "I must help."

Out riding one day he met a leper. Lepers had a terrible disease that covered them with sores. Everyone was frightened of catching it.

Francis was frightened too. But still he lent down, gave the leper money and kissed his hand.

Francis spent a lot of time alone, thinking and praying. Now he knew he must serve his Lord, Jesus, the best way he could.

"But what IS the best way?" he asked himself.

"Priests have rich churches but I should not dare put myself so high when Jesus lived so humbly!"

"Monks have a time for prayer, a place for study, a rule for everything. That is not MY way to God!"

When Francis was about twenty-five, once again a voice spoke to him, this time at the Church of St Damian.

"Repair my house," it said.

"But repairs need money," said Francis.

Without asking, he loaded a horse with reams of fine cloth from his father's shop. Then he sold every bit of the cloth in a nearby town. He sold the horse too.

Francis was pleased but his father wasn't. "Give me all my money back," he raged. "Right now!"

"The money belongs to God and the poor," said Francis.

Even the Bishop of Assisi said he should give the money back.

"Then I shall give back everything," said Francis. "These clothes are my father's, too!"

He put on a servant's robe and chalked a cross on the front. "My only father now is God," said Francis. Then he left.

Two years passed. Francis lived as a poor man, begging for food and walking in the mountains near Assisi.

Many sneered at him. "You have nothing," they said. "You ARE nothing."

"I have everything I need," said Francis. "And I am all I want to be."

23

Francis managed to repair the old church at St Damian, then another, then a third.

By now it was more than three years since Francis had left his family and home.

"There must be more I can do for my Lord than this," Francis thought. "But what?"

"I shall teach others the way of the Lord," said Francis. "And I must live humbly, as He did."

So he gave away the little he had left.

Francis was about twenty-eight now. He began to travel and preach in the towns. People came to listen — a few at first, then more and more...

and even more.

Word was spreading about him.

One very rich and important man, Bernard da Quintavalle, sold everything he had.

He gave all the money to the poor and joined Francis.

Others came too, until there were twelve.

"We twelve shall be friars. We shall travel and preach. We shall care for those we find in need," said Francis. "Our name shall be The Friars Minor."

They went to Rome to ask the Pope, the head of the Catholic Church, to give his approval to their new order of friars.

To Pope Innocent III
The Friars Minor vow to do as the Lord teaches, live simply, own nothing, and never ride on horseback unless we are very sick and cannot walk

More and more people were joining Francis now.

"Think no creature worth less than you," he told them all. "For everything is God's creation!"

"Animals flock around him without fear!" his followers said. "They know how gentle he is."

Francis even composed a poem about all the lovely things of nature.

Francis and his followers became known as Franciscans. Soon there were Franciscans in many countries and friars went to all parts of the world.

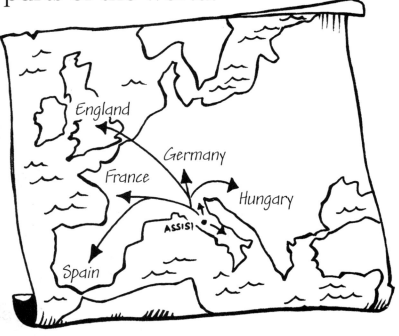

Francis himself went to Egypt although everyone warned him not to.

"You will die there," they said. "Egypt is at war and those Saracens kill Christians!"

But Francis took no notice.

Some Franciscans were finding it hard to live as Francis said they should, though.

"He asks nothing more of us than of himself," said those who supported Francis.

"He is not here," said those who wanted changes. And they started planning.

Francis didn't like what he found back in Italy. A Franciscan convent had been built.

Francis called his followers to listen to him speak.

"Fine buildings and times for prayer are not the Franciscan way," he said.

"I say again. Own nothing. Travel. Live simply and freely. Show your faith above all by love and care for others!"

Francis was forty-two and tired now. "It is time for me to draw closer to my Lord," he said. "Others can look after my friars."

Francis ate nothing and spent his time in prayer. "Have I done enough, Lord?" he said. "If only I could know!"

Then a beautiful vision appeared
before him, both man and angel.
As Francis gazed in wonder, marks
appeared on his own body.

"Wounds just as Our Lord
suffered on the cross," said
Brother Leo.

Francis never showed the marks
given to him by God.

He had little more than two
years left to live now.
He was ill and in great pain.

The Pope's physicians tried to make him better but there was nothing they could do.

"He is dying," they said to each other.

"Take me to Assisi," said Francis.
"I welcome Sister Death."

He was carried to the chapel at
Portiuncula. He broke some
bread and gave a piece to each
friar there.

"I have done my part. May
Christ teach you to do yours,"
he said.

Those were the last words
Francis spoke.

More about Saint Francis

Prayers

Here are a few lines from one of the prayers Francis wrote, still in use by churches today.

Lord, make me an instrument of your peace,
Where there is hatred, let me sow love,
Where there is injury, pardon;
Where there is doubt, faith;
Where there is despair, hope;
Where there is darkness, light;
Where there is sadness, joy. …

The First Nativity

One Christmas Francis set up a little crib scene in a church in Grecchio.

Many people crowded in to hear him preach and saw it. After that, crib scenes became very popular.

Legends

There are many legends told about Francis. One tells how a huge flock of swallows made such a noise he couldn't preach to people in the market place. "Little sisters," said Francis to the birds, "be silent and listen," and they did as he asked! The next day all the birds in the land gathered round him. He blessed them and they flew off in the shape of a cross.

Feast Day

Each October 4th, St Francis is remembered by the Catholic Church.

Some important dates in Saint Francis's lifetime

1181/82 Francis is born in Assisi, Italy.

1202 Francis fights against Perugia and is taken prisoner.

1205 Francis hears a voice at Spoleto telling him to go home.

1209 Francis repairs the little chapel at Portiuncula and begins preaching.

1209/10 The Pope approves the new order of Friars Minor.

1212 Francis helps found the women's order of St Clares.

1219 Francis goes to Egypt and meets with the Sultan.

1224 Francis sees a vision and his body is marked with wounds.

1226 Francis dies peacefully.

1228 Francis is canonised (officially recognised as a saint by the Catholic Church).

1939 Pope Pius XII declares St Francis one of the two patron saints of Italy.